17-80

books by Francis A. Schaeffer

Escape from Reason
The God Who Is There
Death in the City
Pollution and the Death of Man
The Church at the End of the 20th Century
The Mark of the Christian
The Church before the Watching World
He Is There and He Is Not Silent
True Spirituality
Genesis in Space and Time
The New Super-Spirituality
Back to Freedom and Dignity
Basic Bible Studies
Art and the Bible
No Little People
Two Contents, Two Realities
Everybody Can Know (Francis & Edith Schaeffer)

Introduction to
Francis
Schaeffer

study guide to a trilogy:
The God Who Is There, Escape from Reason
& He Is There and He Is Not Silent
plus "How I Have Come to Write My Books"
by Francis A. Schaeffer

InterVarsity Press
Downers Grove, Illinois 60515

InterVarsity Press
is the book publishing
division of Inter-Varsity
Christian Fellowship.

"How I Have Come to Write
My Books" © by L'Abri Fellowship.
Used by permission.

ISBN 0-87784-448-8

Printed in the United
States of America

Introduction

Francis Schaeffer's thought is exerting a significant influence on the church today. Students and professors, pastors and laymen, believers and seekers and skeptics are reading his books, listening to tapes from L'Abri Fellowship and attending his lectures. Many who come in contact with his ideas do so in a rather piecemeal fashion, not realizing that three books lie at the heart of his thought. In a real sense, if these three books are read and understood, the rest of what he writes falls clearly into line as a development of his basic position.

The aim of this guide is to help readers grasp Schaeffer's essential ideas through a study of his "trilogy"—*The God Who Is There* (GWIT). *Escape from Reason* (ER) and *He Is There and He Is Not Silent* (HTHS).

For Individuals and Groups
This guide can be used by either individuals or groups. For an individual it supplies a systematic approach to the three books. If one reads the books in the way suggested by the guide and answers the questions provided, he will have a grasp of the basic essentials of Schaeffer's thought.

For a group, the guide is especially valuable. It provides questions which can stimulate fruitful discussion and keep the group concentrating on major ideas rather than trailing off into tangential issues and personal opinion.

This guide is designed to be used for a twelve-week study of

GWIT, ER and HTHS. If, however, you wish to consider only one of the books, you can use this guide to study GWIT in eight weeks, or ER and HTHS in four weeks each. Because the content of ER fits into the early chapters of GWIT, the first four studies integrate the material in these two books. You can quite easily omit those questions which pertain to the one volume if you wish to study the other.

In sum, then, a group or an individual can use this guide to aid study in all three or any one of the volumes in Francis Schaeffer's trilogy.

The Format of Each Study

Each study has four main parts. First, the purposes are stated to let the reader know its main thrust. Second, the body of the study (which has usually two, sometimes three subheads) directs attention to the text and interprets it in the light of two essential questions: What does the text say? and What does it mean? A third section helps the reader consider the implications of Schaeffer's ideas. Finally, a few sentences summarize the main ideas of the material covered. This summary can be used by a group leader to tie the study together at its conclusion as well as to introduce a session by reminding the group of the content of the previous discussion.

Each study highlights key terms and ideas which appear in Schaeffer's other works. In this way, the guide serves as an introduction to the entire Schaeffer corpus. Also by way of introduction to Schaeffer's works, this guide contains an essay by Schaeffer himself entitled "How I Have Come to Write My Books" (p. 34). This essay may helpfully be read both before the study in the trilogy is undertaken and after it is completed.

If You Are Leading a Group

If you are leading a group, be sure that each member has the books and knows which sections he is to read prior to the first study. (If the members can work through the guide on their own, too, so much the better.) Then work through the study on your own, writing out the answers to each question. Consider which questions you will emphasize and which you will omit if time runs short. As it stands, each study will take at least an hour of discussion. Most likely, you will have to tailor it to suit the needs and time requirements of your particular group.

During each session you have three main responsibilities. First, get the group going. The statement of purpose can help you. Second, guide the group through the body of the study. As you do this, remember to stick to the main theme. Don't let the group get sidetracked. Summarize frequently throughout the discussion to remind people where you have been and where you are heading. Third, summarize the study and be sure everyone knows the assignment for the coming week.

Here are some tips to help you as you lead:

Many of the terms which the group is asked to discuss are defined in the glossary in GWIT. Make sure group members have a chance to state a definition in their own words before you refer to the glossary.

Questions in the guide which call for a yes or no answer should be followed with questions like "Why do you feel that way?" or "What's the reason for your answer?"

If someone quotes a phrase or sentence from the book as an answer to a question, make sure he understands what he has read by asking him, "What does that mean?" or "Could you put that in your own words?"

Do everything you can to encourage balanced discussion. When someone who talks a lot finishes a statement, invite further comment by saying something like, "Does anyone else want to add to that?" or "Does someone have another idea?" Doing this will encourage quieter people to make contributions. But don't be afraid of silences in discussion. If the group is working together, silences can be periods of creative effort. If a silence goes too long, rephrase your question. If someone is continually dominating or silent, talk with him privately about his participation.

If You Are Studying on Your Own

Buy a notebook and write out a complete answer to each question. Set aside a certain amount of time each day and work systematically through the guide.

Here are some tips to help you as you study:

Many of the key terms are defined in the glossary in GWIT. The glossary can help you, but make sure you have formulated a definition in your own words before referring to it.

If the guide asks a question which invites a yes or no answer, be sure to follow your answer with an explanation.

Do not answer a question simply by copying a phrase or sentence from the text. Put the answer in your own words.

Again, remember to read the essay at the end of this book. Then read the first assignment and begin working through the questions.

study 1

The Gulf
Is Fixed

GWIT, chapter 1
ER, chapters 1-2

Purposes
☐ To understand Schaeffer's basic terms and perspective.
☐ To begin studying the intellectual history which has led up to the modern despair.

Introduction (GWIT, chap. 1)
☐ What is the most crucial problem facing Christianity today?
☐ What do these terms mean: *methodology, presuppositions, absolutes, antithesis?* What does this sentence mean: "Absolutes imply antithesis"?
☐ Before "the shift," what were the presuppositions on which both Christians and non-Christians operated?
☐ Define *humanism* and *rationalism.* How is rationalism the unifying factor in non-Christian thought? How are the words *rational* and *rationalism* contrasted?
☐ Why did philosophers depart from the "unified rationalistic circle"? Why did this move them from "rationalistic optimism" to "despair"?
☐ What does Schaeffer mean when he speaks of modern culture being "monolithic" or "uniform"?

Aquinas, Leonardo and the Reformers (ER, chap. 1)
☐ Describe Aquinas's concepts of *nature* and *grace.*

☐ What was his "incomplete view of the biblical Fall"? What main effect did this error have? What various forms has the "sphere of the autonomous" taken?

☐ What does it mean to say that "nature began to 'eat up' grace"? (If time allows, mention some examples in art that illustrate this.)

☐ What hope was Leonardo unwilling to abandon? Why did autonomous rationality threaten this hope?

☐ What was the Reformation answer to the problem of unity? In what two areas did it deny the autonomous?

☐ List some things which we know about man on the basis of God's revelation. (Do not spend much time considering the diagrams on p. 26 because they will be discussed in more detail in a later study.)

Implications

☐ Ask members to review pages 18-19 of GWIT and the foreword of ER. Why is it important for orthodox Christians to understand the intellectual and cultural climate of the second half of the twentieth century? Do *you* believe that such understanding is necessary for effective witness? Since this is a key premise, allow group members to voice and wrestle with any reservations they have.

☐ Ask someone to define a *unified field of knowledge*. Do you personally feel the importance of having a unified perspective? From your own experience or that of a friend, can you share an example of what may happen when a person does not?

☐ Cite a practical difference that having a biblical view of man can or should make in your day-to-day interactions with other people.

Summary

☐ The most crucial problem facing Christianity today is the rationalistic presupposition that truth is known through synthesis rather than through antithesis and that all is therefore relative. This perspective allows no absolutes and no hope for a unified field of knowledge. This way of thinking traces its roots to Aquinas, who was important in the generation of the idea of an autonomous rationality.

study 2

Science and Existentialism

GWIT, chapter 3
ER, chapter 3

Purposes
- ☐ To understand the early development of science.
- ☐ To understand the importance of Hegel and Kierkegaard.
- ☐ To see some of the problems in the secular philosophies which have flowed from Kierkegaard.

Early Modern Science (ER, chap. 3)
- ☐ Why was the biblical mentality necessary to launch modern science?
- ☐ What is the significance of *freedom* replacing *grace* on the diagram on page 33?
- ☐ What was Rousseau's fear? How did he combat it?
- ☐ What do these terms mean: *uniformity of natural causes in an open system* (the premise of modern science) and *uniformity of natural causes in a closed system* (the premise of modern modern science)? Why was the shift in science from belief in one to belief in the other so significant? Why in the latter can unity be achieved only by ruling out freedom, love and other values (see diagram, p. 37)?
- ☐ What effect does the premise of modern modern science have on morals?

Hegel and Kierkegaard (ER, pp. 40-45; GWIT, pp. 20-22)
- ☐ In what two areas did Hegel change "the rules of the game" (ER,

p. 41)? How did he change them?

☐ Why can Kierkegaard be thought of as the father of both modern secular thinking and the new theological thinking (GWIT, p. 21)?

☐ Describe the dichotomy he created (see diagram, GWIT, p. 22).

☐ In what three ways did Kierkegaard's new way of thinking spread (ER, pp. 43-44)?

☐ Why is this way of thinking *despair* (ER, p. 45)?

Secular Existentialist Philosophies (GWIT, pp. 22-30)

☐ What problems does Schaeffer see in the "final experience" of Jaspers? the "authentication" of Sartre and Heidegger?

☐ Define each of the following and discuss the problems inherent in it: (1) logical positivism, (2) defining philosophy, (3) evolutionary humanism, (4) serious drug taking.

☐ What is *the mannishness of man*? Why is it important?

Implications

☐ Is there an inherent conflict between Christianity and science? Is it valid for a Christian to be a scientist?

☐ What are some current manifestations of the philosophy "What *is* is right"? What steps can we take to combat them?

☐ Hegel and Kierkegaard caused a communication gap: "The reason why Christians are not understanding their own children is because the children are being educated into the other way of thinking" (ER, p. 44). What steps can both age groups take to eliminate this gap?

Summary

☐ The premise of the uniformity of natural causes in an open system generated modern science. The premise of the uniformity of natural causes in a closed system generated modern modern science. Hegel introduced the notion of knowing through synthesis; Kierkegaard, concluding that we cannot arrive at synthesis by reason, introduced the leap of faith and took men below the line of despair. Many current, inadequate philosophies have flowed from these two men.

study 3

Below the Line
of Despair

GWIT, chapters 3-4
ER, chapters 4-6

Purposes
☐ To review some basic concepts.
☐ To study some illustrations of the tension of modern man.
☐ To begin considering the New Theology.

Review (ER, chap.4)
☐ What is the *upper story? the lower story?* What is significant about the fact that a gap exists between them? What are some examples of upper story experiences?
☐ After philosophy went below the line of despair, what other disciplines followed it and in what order (see diagram, ER, p. 43)?

Despair in Art, Music and General Culture
(GWIT, chaps. 3-4; ER, pp. 58-73)
☐ Since we do not have time to discuss all the examples Schaeffer gives, we will focus only on some of the men and movements who have gone below the line of despair in art, music and other areas of culture. (If possible, display reproductions of some of the artists' works, especially those works mentioned in the text.)
☐ Who are the three pillars of modern art? What were they all trying to discover?
☐ What problem does Picasso's art exhibit? Why was his "solution"

a failure?

☐ Why is Marcel Duchamp important?

☐ When discussing musique concrète, Schaeffer says, *"There can be no other terminus [than chaos] when antithesis dies, when relativism is born and when the possibility of finding any universal which would make sense of the particulars is denied"* (GWIT, p. 38). What does this mean?

☐ In the second diagram on page 66 of ER, why does the lower story contain the words *man is dead*?

☐ What are the three steps in the Theatre of the Absurd?

The New Theology (ER, pp. 50-53, 73-79)

☐ Why was Karl Barth's view of Scripture important?

☐ Discuss the way the New Theology uses words (pp. 52-53).

☐ Why did the New Theology lead logically to the conclusion that God is dead? Relate your answer to the fact that in the New Theology faith is unverifiable.

☐ How has the word *Jesus* become the enemy of the Person Jesus?

Implications

☐ What options for upper story experiences are being offered today?

☐ Give specific examples of contemporary paintings, films, music, mass media, etc., that communicate a message of despair. How can we combat these destructive influences?

☐ What can Christians do to see that the proper content is retained in the word *Jesus*?

Summary

☐ Accepting the notion that a gap exists between the upper and lower stories, modern man has gone below the line of despair in art, music, general culture and theology. The New Theology is a manifestation of the resultant upper story mysticism.

study 4

Rationality
and Faith

GWIT, chapter 5
ER, chapter 7

Purposes
☐ To consider the relation of rationality and faith.
☐ To discuss the Christian response to people under the line of despair.

Rationality and Faith (ER, chap. 7)
☐ What are some consequences of putting Christianity in the upper story?
☐ Why is it necessary to hold the full Reformation view of Scripture? to affirm the lordship of Christ in every area of life?
☐ What does this sentence mean: "Any autonomy is wrong"?
☐ What is the relation between *form* and *freedom*?
☐ How does the Bible provide a justification for man's beginning with himself in his search for truth?
☐ What is the consequence of believing that man was produced by the impersonal, plus time, plus chance?
☐ What *is* the Bible (p. 89)? (Discuss the meaning of the following: *verbalized propositional communication from God to man, in a definite, historic, space-time situation.*)
☐ Discuss briefly the Jewish, Greek and modern views of truth.
☐ What two things must Christians grasp in order to communicate the gospel to non-Christians today?

The Christian Response (GWIT, chap. 5)

☐ What main idea is reiterated on pages 44-45?

☐ What is the good side of the fact that so many people live under the line of despair?

☐ How is Christianity "realistic"? compassionate?

☐ How does Christianity differ from optimistic humanism? from nihilism?

☐ Read the definition of *dialectic* in the GWIT glossary. Why must Christians oppose the dialectic methodology?

Implications

☐ Why is *Escape from Reason* titled *Escape from Reason*? In what system can rationality legitimately operate? Why?

☐ This study highlights the importance of the ideational, or conceptual, aspect of life (that is, of beliefs). How can you ensure that Jesus is Lord of your intellectual life? If you are a Christian student, how should your faith affect the way you relate your course assignments to each other? If you are working, how should your faith affect the way you integrate your work, family and social activities?

☐ How can we "consciously build back the mentality of antithesis among Christians" (GWIT, p. 47)?

Summary

☐ The Reformation view of Scripture provides a system in which rationality can legitimately operate. Holding this view enables Christians to bring every area of life under the lordship of Christ and to respond appropriately (with realism and compassion) to twentieth-century people.

study 5

The New Theology

GWIT, section II

Purpose

☐ To study the New Theology in more detail.

Departure from Biblical Christianity

☐ Why must one understand the New Theology *as a system*?

☐ How did the naturalistic theologians fail?

☐ After their failure, what two things could they have done to continue in a rational and logical realm?

☐ What third way did they choose? Why? (In addition to the two reasons given on p. 52, consider the italicized statement on the bottom of p. 58.)

Despair beyond Despair

☐ Why is the modern dichotomy of reason and meaning worse than simple nihilism?

☐ What is the third level of despair?

☐ What has the New Theology done to the word *symbol*?

☐ How and why has the New Theology successfully deceived many people?

☐ How is the "faith" of modern theology different from Christian "faith"? (See also appendix 2 in HTHS.)

☐ Identify each of these men and explain briefly how he is an example of "modern mysticism in action": Paul Klee, Salvador Dali, the later Heidegger, Leonard Bernstein, John Cage and Henry Miller.

God Is Dead, or He Is Everything

☐ The New Theology's attempt to breach the dichotomy of the two stories has taken two forms. What are they?

☐ What attempts are "the upper story men" making to "get a toe back into history"?

☐ Why is the present moment a time of great opportunity for the New Theology?

Implications

☐ What effects has the New Theology had on individuals or churches you know? How can Schaeffer's analysis help you respond to them?

☐ What role is the New Theology playing in society today? Have Schaeffer's fears about its growing influence been realized?

☐ What can Christians do to prepare themselves and their children against "manipulated semantic mysticism"?

Summary

☐ Christians must understand the New Theology as a system because its basic concept of truth is wrong. Therefore, what "sounds right" may simply be manipulated semantic mysticism rather than historic Christian faith. The New Theology, in attempting to breach the dichotomy of the two stories, has in fact led men either to pantheism or atheism.

study 6

Historic Christianity

GWIT, section III

Purposes
☐ To see how historic Christianity differs from the New Theology.
☐ To consider how one can know that Christianity (or any system)
is true.

Three Great Differences
☐ The first great difference between historic Christianity and the
New Theology regards the reality of individual personality. What is
the difference in the two perspectives?
☐ What is Christianity's explanation for the source and meaning of
personality?
☐ What is the logical end of denying personality?
☐ The second great difference between historic Christianity and
the New Theology is that the latter gives no basis for verifiable facts
and knowing. Why is the possibility of verifiable facts consistent with
the biblical position? Why does the Christian system have an adequate basis for the unity of knowledge? Why is the New Theology
deficient at this point?
☐ What is the difference between saying that God communicates
exhaustively and that God communicates *truly*?
☐ What does the diagram on page 94 mean? How is the one on page
95 different?
☐ Why is it that Christianity can make *love* more than a word? How

should this fact change my perspective on human relationships?

☐ The third great difference between historic Christianity and the New Theology is their explanation of man's dilemma. What is the essential difference in these explanations?

☐ What four important facts flow from the biblical answer?

How Do We Know It Is True?

☐ Ask someone to explain the torn book analogy on pages 108-09.

☐ What two steps are involved in proof?

☐ What four possible explanations of reality does Schaeffer discuss which do not meet these two criteria? How does each one fail?

Implications

☐ How can knowing that God has communicated truly free us to learn more about his world? (See especially pp. 93 and 112-13.)

☐ Schaeffer makes clear that a Christian has a basis for fighting evil. Identify a social evil you would like to combat. What specific steps could you take to do so?

☐ What impresses you most about Christianity's ability to be proven? What problems bother you most? (Be sensitive to any doubts group members express. Try to deal with them in private conversation or in future group discussions.)

Summary

☐ Contrary to the New Theology, historic Christianity has (1) an adequate and reasonable explanation for the source and meaning of personality, (2) a basis for verifiable facts and knowing, and (3) a true explanation of man's dilemma that provides hope. Historic Christianity also meets the two criteria of proof.

study 7

Communicating Christianity

GWIT, sections III and IV

Purposes
☐ To discover how to communicate Christianity to modern man.
☐ To consider the importance of Christian apologetics and the Christian concept of truth.

Finding the Point of Tension
☐ What attitude should a Christian have toward a non-Christian with whom he wants to communicate?
☐ Why is a non-Christian a person in tension?
☐ What does Schaeffer mean when he says that everyone has stopped "somewhere along the line" between the real world and the logical conclusions of his presuppositions?
☐ What, then, is the "first consideration in our apologetics for modern man"?
☐ After a Christian has discovered a non-Christian's point of tension, what is his next step?
☐ At what point should he stop talking about presuppositions?
☐ What three things must a person understand before he is ready to become a Christian?
☐ To use Schaeffer's other terminology, what does it mean to *take the roof off*? Why is this an appropriate step in witnessing to people who are under the line of despair?
☐ How can Christians dare take this approach in evangelism?

□ In what two ways must a person bow to exercise Christian faith?
□ According to the four questions on pages 134-35, what essential content must a person affirm to "believe on the Lord Jesus"?

The Importance of Truth
□ What are the two purposes of Christian apologetics? Why is each important?
□ Discuss the significance of this statement: "Knowledge precedes faith."
□ Why must truth come first in conversion? in true spirituality?
□ What is the significance of speaking of *the God who is there*?

Implications
□ Ask two people to role play a situation in which a Christian finds a non-Christian's point of tension, takes the roof off and gives the person an opportunity to believe in Christ. (You may want to have this rehearsed ahead of time.) Then evaluate the role play by Schaeffer's principles.
□ Think of a person to whom you have been witnessing or to whom you can witness. What do you suspect may be his point of tension? What specific steps can you take to communicate Christianity to him?
□ Mention some things your church can do to ensure that its children will not be lost to Christianity because they are turned off by the attitude, "Don't ask questions. Just have faith."

Summary
□ To communicate Christianity to modern man, a Christian should discover where a person has stopped on the line between the real world and the logical conclusions of his own non-Christian presuppositions (that is, find his point of tension), push him toward the logical conclusions of his presuppositions and give the gospel's solution to him as soon as he is ready to hear it. To become a Christian, a non-Christian must bow to God metaphysically and morally and affirm the essential content of the gospel. To further the cause of Christ, Christians should be able to defend Christianity and communicate it in a way the contemporary generation understands.

study 8

The Practice
of Truth

GWIT, section VI and appendices

Purpose
☐ To consider why practicing Christian truth is important and how it can be done.

Substantial Healing
☐ A Christian must face the same question as a non-Christian. What is it (see diagram, p. 151)?

☐ What four divisions did the Fall cause?

☐ Why does Schaeffer speak of *substantial* healing of the last three divisions?

☐ What is *the final apologetic*? How is it accomplished?

☐ What should be a Christian's attitude toward perfection?

☐ What effect should recognizing the personal nature of the universe have on a Christian (pp. 156-57)? Why?

☐ How is the new birth "everything" yet "very little"?

☐ Why should Christians be "both individually and corporately living on a personal level"?

☐ What are the three ways of judging a work of art? Why is this a human, personal approach?

☐ What theological truth is the basis for a Christian's involvement in culture?

☐ With what two things must Christian education constantly and consciously be wrestling?

Building the Church

☐ What two groups is the orthodox evangelical church failing to reach?

☐ What three principles must it implement to reach them?

☐ How can proper use of these principles be helpful to the church itself?

☐ As Christians seek to apply these principles, what two things must they avoid?

☐ What two concepts should the church keep in mind as it trains young people to take their part in Christian work?

☐ What is the central problem of evangelical orthodoxy in the second half of the twentieth century? In what two areas is the absence of truth and antithesis especially acute?

Implications

☐ In your present experience, which of the four divisions caused by the Fall do you feel most acutely? What basis does the Bible supply for substantial healing in this area?

☐ Give an example of how the lordship of Christ touches a "non-religious" aspect of your life. Are you aware of any areas where you are not living under the lordship of Christ?

☐ At which one of the three points listed on page 163 do you feel your own church or Christian group most falls short? What can you do about this?

Summary

☐ If the church wants to reach the unreached, Christian truth must be practiced as well as proclaimed. Substantial healing of the divisions caused by the Fall is possible.

study 9

The Metaphysical Necessity

HTHS, chapter 1

Purposes

☐ To consider the basic answers given to the basic philosophical questions.

☐ To consider why only Christianity has an adequate answer for the metaphysical problem of existence.

Basic Answers to Basic Questions

☐ Identify and define the three basic areas of philosophic thought.

☐ In discussing epistemology, what two observations does Schaeffer make about philosophy (pp. 3-4)?

☐ What are the two classes of answers to basic philosophic questions?

☐ Why can't someone who holds the first answer act consistently with it?

☐ Those who believe that there is an answer which can be rationally and logically considered must explain why something (rather than nothing) is there. What three final options do they have for doing this? Why does Schaeffer speak of *nothing nothing*? What problem does *paneverythingism* fail to solve? Why is dualism also an insufficient answer (see footnote, p. 19)? How does the Christian answer speak to the heart of modern man's dilemma?

God or gods?

☐ What two things are needed in order to have an adequate answer for a personal beginning (hence, for the metaphysical problem of existence)?

☐ Why is "only a personal-infinite God . . . big enough"?

☐ What problem is avoided by the fact that God is triune? What problem is solved?

☐ What is the significance of saying that the *full biblical answer* is *true to what is there*?

☐ Why can Schaeffer maintain "It is the Christian answer or nothing"?

Implications

☐ To tell twentieth-century people that they have significance is both (1) legitimate evangelism and (2) active love. Why?

☐ Recall or imagine a discussion with someone who holds that there is no logical, rational answer to metaphysical problems. Summarize what a Christian should communicate to him.

☐ Next, recall or imagine a conversation with someone who believes the universe did not have a personal beginning. Formulate a Christian response.

☐ Finally, repeat this process imagining someone who believes in some sort of "limited gods."

Summary

☐ In the area of being and existence, the fact that God is there and is not silent is a necessity. This alone gives an adequate answer for a personal beginning, namely, a personal-infinite God who exists on the high order of trinity.

study 10

The Moral
Necessity

HTHS, chapter 2

Purposes
☐ To understand the moral implications of affirming that the universe had an impersonal beginning.
☐ To consider the two explanations that can be given for man's cruelty if one affirms that the universe had a personal beginning.

An Impersonal Beginning
☐ If the universe had an impersonal beginning, why do man's finiteness and his cruelty (metaphysics and morals) become the same thing?
☐ Define *moral motions.* What does a belief in an impersonal beginning plus a feeling of moral motions lead to?
☐ To the pantheist, what is the final tension?
☐ If the universe had an impersonal beginning, what is the final status of cruelty and non-cruelty, right and wrong?

A Personal Beginning
☐ If an individual affirms a personal beginning, in what two ways can he explain man's cruelty?
☐ What two problems does a person face if he believes that man has always been as he now is?
☐ What two tensions are set up as soon as a person *irrationally* affirms that God is good?

☐ How does the Judaeo-Christian position explain man's cruelty?

☐ What four things emerge from saying that because of moral guilt man is abnormal?

☐ Why, in the area of morals, is it important that God has spoken?

☐ Why is the death of Christ important?

☐ Why is the *word* "God" not in itself sufficient?

Implications

☐ Why must Christians begin by emphasizing that God is personal if they hope to combat situational, relativistic ethics?

☐ Why is it important for Christians to affirm a historic, space-time Fall?

☐ On the basis of this chapter, list the things for which you can praise and thank God. (After the list is completed would be a good time for the group to pray together.)

Summary

☐ If a person believes that the universe had an impersonal beginning, he has no basis for morality. If one believes that the universe had a personal beginning, he can explain man's cruelty by affirming either that man has always been what he now is or that man is now abnormal. The former explanation creates insoluble problems; the latter (as the Judaeo-Christian position expresses it) is livable because Christ's substitutionary death provides a solution and also because man can hope and work for change.

study 11

The Epistemological Necessity: The Problem

HTHS, chapter 3

Purposes
☐ To see the relation of modern culture to its historical antecedents.

☐ To understand the epistemological dilemma of modern society (by discussing the significance of *silence*).

Modern Culture and Its Antecedents
☐ What is the heart of the problem of epistemology?

☐ Summarize briefly the intellectual history described on pages 37-47 (much of which is repeated from ER and GWIT), being sure to mention the Greeks, Aquinas, Leonardo, modern science and modern modern science, Rousseau, Hegel and Kierkegaard.

☐ What is the significance of the imagined conversation between Rousseau and the Greeks (p. 45)?

☐ How does the modern culture relate to the above history? What is the essence of the modern perspective? Base your answers on page 45, paragraph 3; page 47, paragraph 1; page 48, paragraph 2; and page 54, paragraph 2 (last two sentences).

☐ What is *positivism*? What problem in it did Polanyi point out? What further problems does Schaeffer see?

Silence
☐ Why is Wittgenstein associated with *silence*?

☐ How do Wittgenstein and Heidegger differ? What do they have in common?

☐ What four categories are affected by cynicism about knowing? How are they affected?

☐ How does man's present state differ from the one for which he was intended? Why?

Implications

☐ Schaeffer stresses that the lack of universals is even more important in the area of knowledge than in the area of morals. Why do you think he feels this way?

☐ What specific differences would it make in your life if you were to live tomorrow believing there are no universals?

☐ If we truly "weep for our generation," what specific steps can we take to express our concern about its epistemological dilemma?

Summary

☐ Because of the influence of past thinkers (especially Rousseau, Kant, Hegel and Kierkegaard), our culture has become cynical about knowing. Instead of experiencing the fellowship with God and other people for which he was intended, modern man experiences *silence*.

study 12

The Epistemological Necessity: The Answer

HTHS, chapter 4

Purposes
☐ To understand why Christianity has no problem of epistemology.
☐ To see three results that flow from this.

Why Christianity Has No Problem of Epistemology
☐ Why did the Reformation have no nature-grace problem?
☐ Why does the presupposition of the uniformity of natural causes in a closed system rule out the biblical position? Why is this presupposition of the uniformity of natural causes in a closed system not acceptable?
☐ What are the basic Christian presuppositions? Given these presuppositions, why is it not nonsensical to say that God could communicate propositionally (see p. 66 and appendix 1)?
☐ Why does Schaeffer predict the death of silence?
☐ Why does the Christian viewpoint not have the subject-object problem?
☐ What view of language is consistent with the Christian structure?

Three Results of the Christian View
☐ How is the Christian different from both modern man and Eastern man regarding the relation of knowledge and fantasy?
☐ Why can a Christian "live in the world God has made"?

☐ In what two ways does the Bible teach truth?

☐ Because men have lost the objective basis of certainty of knowledge, in what two ways is science becoming a game?

☐ How does the Christian view of epistemology affect interpersonal relations?

☐ Why can biblical teaching bring increasing integration of the inward and outward man?

☐ Why is a Christian free to use his imagination?

☐ Summarize HTHS (and the entire trilogy) by discussing this question: Why is it so important that God is not silent?

Implications

☐ How should the information in this chapter affect your interactions with non-Christians? with Christians?

☐ Are you personally experiencing the results that flow from the Christian answer to the epistemological question? For instance, do you feel you are experiencing the gradual integration about which Schaeffer speaks? Do you feel free to express yourself creatively? If not, how can Schaeffer's perspective help and encourage you?

☐ In what way do you think these studies in Francis Schaeffer's thought have most changed you?

Summary

☐ Christianity has no problem of epistemology because God made the universe, made man to live in that universe and gave the Bible (verbalized revelation) to tell man what he needs to know. As a result, a Christian can look outward and understand why there is a subject-object relationship. He can look at another man and know that that man is made in the image of God. And, because he can distinguish between reality and fantasy, he can be "the man with flaming imagination."

"How I Have Come to Write My Books"

Over the past few years my wife Edith and I have been carrying out a comprehensive program of writing. At present, nineteen books of ours have come out of our ministry at L'Abri. To explain why I write, I have to go back to my late teens.

For some time I attended a very liberal church. Sunday after Sunday I listened to the minister, and the more I listened the more I realized that he was giving answers to nothing. Finally I could go on with this no longer, and I became an agnostic.

In my search for answers I read and studied all the philosophy I could find. I even went back into the time of the Greeks. While reading Ovid one night, I thought, "Well now, I'm reading all this material; maybe I should read the Bible, too—just as a matter of curiosity and honesty." So I began to read. Each night I read a little from Ovid and a little from the Bible. I never finished reading that particular book of Ovid, but I have read the Bible I don't know how many times since.

I found truth in that Book. In my reading of philosophy I saw that there were innumerable problems that nobody was giving answers for. But in the Bible I began to find answers, not merely individual answers that shot down the problems one at a time, but even though I was finite it put a cable in my hand which bound all the problems together and gave a systematic answer to them. The Bible, it struck me, dealt with man's problems in a sweeping, all-encompassing thrust.

In about six months I was flattened. At the beginning of that period, I was not a Christian. I don't know exactly when the change came, but I know that at the end of those six months I was a Christian.

What this experience did was to give me a total confidence in the Bible. Since then I have studied it for over forty years. Today I know a lot more about the intellectual problems and the problems of the world, and yet every year I become more convinced that the Bible, when it is read as it is written, gives the answers to all the intellectual questions and to all of life.

The way to read my books, then, is to realize that I came through a real struggle in those early days and that I've tried to be honest in my study ever since. I try to approach every problem as though I were not a Christian and see what the answer would be.

Later on in my ministry I faced another crisis that equally influenced the writing of my books. It came after I had already been a pastor in the U.S. for ten years and a missionary to Europe for five years. Throughout this period one thing was dinned into my thinking: "Why," I asked, "is there so little reality among orthodox evangelical Christians? Why is there so little beauty in the way Christians deal with one another?"

This led to doubts about the reality of spiritual things in my own life. I realized that although I had been studying for years and although I had been active in Christian ministry and although I was becoming more and more known in certain Christian circles, the reality of my own spiritual life was less than it had been when I was a young Christian.

For about two months I walked in the Swiss mountains, and prayed and thought. When it rained, I walked in the old hayloft above our chalet. And as I prayed, I went all the way back to my agnosticism. With as much honesty as I could, I asked myself, "Was I right in becoming a Christian?" The unreality I had found in the Christian world, the ugliness I saw in all too many Christian relationships, the fact that Christians were not able to talk to twentieth-century people—all these things made me ask, "Was I right?"

Finally the sun came out. I saw that my earlier decision to step from agnosticism to Bible-believing Christianity was right, and I also discovered that I had been missing something vital in my biblical understanding. It was this: that the finished work of Christ on the cross, back there in time and space, has a moment-by-moment, present meaning. Christ meant his promise to be taken literally when he said that he would bear his fruit through us if we allowed him to do so, not only in our religious life but in all of our life. This brought my life to a great shattering moment. What began as struggle ended in a song. Without that crisis, I could never have written *True Spirituality*, for that book is the outcome of that personal struggle.

This, then, was the background when, in 1955, my wife and I with our children began L'Abri in the little village of Huemoz, Switzerland. Edith and I committed ourselves to God with one aim. It was not an evangelistic work we wished to start nor a young people's work nor a work for intellectuals nor an outreach to drug people. It was simply that we offered ourselves to God and asked him if he would use us to demonstrate that he exists in our generation. That's all L'Abri is; that's the way it began.

Some of my friends at that time scolded me thoroughly. Why should I limit myself to talking to so few people? Humanly speaking, it was a moment of sacrifice. In some small way, it was the grain of wheat falling into the ground and dying.

At L'Abri, I listened as well as talked. I learned something more about twentieth-century thinking in many fields, across many disciplines. Gradually, people began to come from the ends of the earth—not only students but professors and others. They heard that L'Abri was a place where one could discuss the twentieth-century questions quite openly. To the best of my ability I gave the Bible's answers. But all the time I tried to listen and learn the thought forms of these people. I think that my knowledge, whatever it is, is formed from two factors: (1) forty years of hard study and (2) trying to listen to the twentieth-century man as he talked.

I still had no thought of writing books. As more and more people came, someone sent us a tape recorder. My reaction was, "Thank you very much, but I'll never work with a tape recorder."

One day we were having a bang-up conversation with some Smith College girls, all of them really bright girls, agnostic or atheistic. All of a sudden I noticed one of our workers fooling with the flowers, and I thought, "I wonder what he's up to." What he was up to was hiding a microphone. Later, the girls, instead of being put off as I thought they might be, all wanted copies of the tape. That was the unplanned beginning of our tape program. At the present time, I have about 1300-1400 hours on tape and there are many more hours by the other members of the L'Abri staff.

At the same time I was being invited to lecture in wider and wider circles: Cambridge, Oxford, Fribourg, University of London, Manchester. I never wanted to stand in a privileged position where I couldn't be answered so I threw the meetings open for discussion.

As I listened, I continued to learn what contemporary thought forms really were, and I learned how to present the gospel to the twentieth-century man so that it was clear to him. And gradually a message came forward which I began to use in various places. I called it "Speaking Historic Christianity into the Twentieth-Century World." I gave this lecture at a number of universities, including Harvard and MIT. After I presented it at Wheaton College, they put it out in pamphlet form. That was the first thing to come out in print. When I saw that this was really a rather extensive piece, I knew I had in my hands something the Lord could use to give the gospel to my own generation.

So we took it to a publisher in England. We decided to call it *The God Who Is There*. It was written in such a way that it would fit two groups. It would fit the non-Christian so that he could hear the gospel in his own terms, and it would also fit the Christian who wished to speak to the twentieth-century person. At first the publishers said, "But we don't know what reading public it's for." Nevertheless, they went ahead, and I thank God that it has reached into both groups. That was 1968.

Wrongly—perhaps because it was shorter—many people have assumed that *Escape from Reason* is the "introduction" and *The God Who Is There* a development of it. In fact, the opposite is the truth. *The God Who Is There* was written first; it lays the groundwork, establishes the terminology and sets out the basic thesis. We at L'Abri have attempted to show that Christianity has balance: that biblical exegesis gives intellectual depth, and also, in the area of practical living and beauty, Christianity has a relation to the whole man. Beginning with the Christian system as God has given it to men in the verbalized propositional revelation of the Bible, one can move along and find that every area of life is touched by truth and a song. *Escape from Reason* works out this principle particularly in the philosophical area of Nature and Grace, and shows how modern culture has grown from polluted roots far back in the late Middle Ages.

After these two books perhaps *He Is There and He Is Not Silent* should have been published. That would have been its logical place, but I worked for five more years before feeling it was ready in its final form. The three make a unified base; without them the various applications in the other books are really suspended in space. *He Is There and He Is Not Silent* deals with one of the most fundamental of all questions: how we know, and how we know we know. Unless our epistemology is right, everything is going to be wrong. That is why it goes with *The God Who Is There*—a link emphasized by its title. The infinite-personal God is there, but also he is not silent and that changes the whole world.

On the base of these three books, which constitute a conscious unity (a unity which I believe rests on the unity of Scripture itself), all the other books which have come or will come depend. These three books are the hub, the other books the spokes radiating out from them. They apply this unified Christian system to various areas. It should be noted that *The God Who Is There* has two appendices which deal with two specific problems: the middle-class church in the twentieth century and the practice of truth in Christian work and evangelism. These are developed in the later books. *Death in the City* is exegetical, picking up the application of the earlier books to American and Northern European culture as it has turned away from what God has given us as a base—as it has deliberately thrown away the Christian consensus upon which it was built.

Next came *Pollution and the Death of Man,* the Christian answer to the ecological dilemma, based on the same consistent system. *The Church at the End of the 20th Century* moved into other areas of application—sociology and ecclesiology. The two appendices to that book, *Adultery and Apostasy* and *The Mark of the Christian* (also published as a separate small book) picked up the theme touched on in the second appendix to *The God Who Is There:* They emphasize the balance to be struck between the practice of the purity of the visible church and the love which ought to mark relationships between all true Christians, no matter what their differences are. There is also a fuller and practical treatment of ecclesiology in *The Church before the Watching World*.

It might be alleged that this is merely a new, arid scholasticism, applied in the areas of epistemology, ecclesiology, ecology, sociology and so forth. If it were, then it would be nothing but a tinkling cymbal. Five books, however, redress the balance. The last chapter of *Death in the City*, "The Universe and Two Chairs," is important here. Edith's book, *L'Abri*, is a vital element, and without it the other books lack true unity and balance. Her book shows how acting upon the fact that the infinite-personal God is really there has worked out in day-by-day practice in the community of L'Abri. *True Spirituality* is likewise crucial; it is a systematic treatment of the whole basis of a Christian's living in an open relationship with God and then with himself and others. *Everybody Can Know* and *No Little People* also fit here though they were written later. Edith's book *Hidden Art* has an important place as it carries these matters into the practical and beautiful area of creativity in the Christian's life.

At this point in my writing and publishing I felt that a balance had finally been achieved. Between Edith and myself, books emphasizing both the intellectual and the practical aspects of the Christian life had been produced. Now we turned to a development of some of the themes introduced by our previous books but as yet not treated as fully as we wished.

Genesis in Space and Time picked up themes in *The God Who Is There* and focused attention on the necessity to take biblical, space-time history seriously—all the way back through the first eleven chapters of Genesis. The two long footnotes in this book I think are as important as anything I have written about the danger of modern evangelicalism becoming less than evangelical. In addition, it gave a more fully developed exegetical base to the decisive point of beginnings. *Back to Freedom and Dignity* picked up a theme in *The Church at the End of the 20th Century* and examined recent trends in genetics, psychology and physiology that are bent on treating man in purely mechanistic terms. *The New Super-Spirituality* examined the opposite tendency among Christians, in short, to see the Christian life in solely super-rational terms, lacking an adequate content.

In *Art and the Bible* I wanted to counter the tendency among Christians to write off the world of art. One of its two essays explains something of the artistic work God commanded ancient Israel to do, and the other essay suggests eleven perspectives within which a Christian view of art can take shape. *Basic Bible Studies* publishes Bible studies developed over many years and used through the years in L'Abri with people of all levels of education. *Everybody Can Know,* which Edith and I did together, is a study of Luke written to be read out loud to all ages. It is for the whole family. And our hope is that this book will help carry the things we have written into the next generation.

The most recent books to appear are *No Little People: Sixteen Sermons for the Twentieth Century* and *Two Contents, Two Realities.* The former is a compilation of sermons that have been preached in the chapel at L'Abri. Many have also been delivered during speaking engagements in Europe, the United States and in other parts of the world. *Two Contents, Two Realities* summarizes what I would most like to say to contemporary evangelical Christians all over the world— that genuine evangelism is nothing short of the full Christian life composed of sound doctrine and the practice of that doctrine, the giving of honest answers to honest questions, true spirituality, and a beauty of human relationships, especially as carried out in the practice of community in Christian churches and groups. Anything less is a distortion of the character and message of true Christianity.

Looking back over this list of books makes me realize how much we seem to have thrust on the reading public. Still, I know from people who suddenly appear at my home in Switzerland, others whom I meet in correspondence and as I travel that God has used these books in many parts of the world and over a wide spectrum of people. We are deeply thankful. It is our prayer that God will continue to so use them.

DATE DUE